YOUR KNOWLEDGE HAS

Bibliographic information published by the German National Library:

The German National Library lists this publication in the National Bibliography; detailed bibliographic data are available on the Internet at http://dnb.dnb.de .

Imprint:

Copyright © 2018 GRIN Verlag
Print and binding: Books on Demand GmbH, Norderstedt Germany
ISBN: 9783668668843

This book at GRIN:

https://www.grin.com/document/416755

Manisha Kumari Deep

Cloud Computing. DDoS, Blockchain, Regulation and Compliance

GRIN Verlag

GRIN - Your knowledge has value

Since its foundation in 1998, GRIN has specialized in publishing academic texts by students, college teachers and other academics as e-book and printed book. The website www.grin.com is an ideal platform for presenting term papers, final papers, scientific essays, dissertations and specialist books.

Visit us on the internet:

http://www.grin.com/

http://www.facebook.com/grincom

http://www.twitter.com/grin_com

CLOUD: DDoS, BLOCKCHAIN, REGULATION AND COMPLAINCE

Dr. Manisha Kumari Deep

Summary

Cloud computing is a promising technology where computational power is provided over internet as per users demand just like the supplies daily utilities of tap water, electricity and gas provided as pay per use. The features of easy accessibility anywhere at any time and almost no burden of on-going operational expenses like running of data-centre makes it one of the fastest growing technologies with the overall business of cloud being anticipated to be above $40 billion by 2012. The popularity of cloud computing and its growing reach poses some unanswered questions regarding security and authentication of both the user and the provider. How much a user can rely on the cloud service provider for data security and application related services? In 2009 NIST defined Cloud Computing as "a model for enabling convenient, on-demand network access to a shared pool of configurable computing resources that can be rapidly provisioned and released with minimal management effort or service provider interaction [3]. With the growing number of organizations moving towards cloud platform, issues like security, compliance, threats, attacks and intrusion are some of the most challenging and unresolved issues. Due to low cost, scalability, elasticity, sharing of resources, global presence and ease of business, more and more firms are moving towards cloud computing technology. Cloud compliance is a nagging problem with firms or users using cloud backup or storage facility. With more and more research being done, several problem areas in cloud computing were identified that were blocking the widespread adoption of cloud on the enterprise level, are listed below [22]:

- Security and privacy

- Controllability and flexibility

- Visibility and availability

- Auditability and accountability

- Latency, performance/throughput

- Compliance

Here I have attempted to provide solutions to some of the above stated problems. Two emerging cloud deployment models and two emerging cloud service models have also been briefly discussed. DDoS attacks have been listed and effects discussed along with an alternated solution for Blockchain DDoS attacks. Though data protection laws can be different with change in jurisdiction but here emphasis has been given on data policies existing in India based on IT Act (2000). In case of data transfer or storage the data protection laws of both the jurisdiction any intermediate jurisdiction has to be taken into consideration. Compliance with the involved jurisdictions at state or country level becomes mandatory for the organizations or users involved in data transfer/storage/retrieval/deletion/updating/management. Important points of consideration have been listed for organizations to consider while designing SLA's and their compliance Strategy. IT Act (2000) has been discussed here and Strategies to be designed keeping the omissions in mind. National law regulating the collection and use of personal data is the Information Technology Act 2000 (IT Act) has been stated and suggestions provided to safeguard data in case of data storage, retrieval, deletion or transfer. Dynamic Trust Management Method (DTMM) has been discussed in context to Cloud and Blockchain. Finally a reference model has been suggested for avoiding DDoS and Blockchain DDoS Attacks in Cloud Environment. Finally the discussions has been concluded highlighting the recommendations and necessary actions needed for the same.

Cloud

Cloud platform provides access to applications and software from anywhere as per need to the user. This means storage and power is no more a user's problem while they are working in a cloud environment. Before cloud computing came into existence a whole team of experts were needed for installing, configuring, testing, managing, updating and securing the hardware and software used for running applications for business enterprises. So this made business applications pretty expensive. But with the introduction of cloud computing's pay per use model, business applications have been made available at much affordable cost also simultaneously optimizing resources and improving scalability. But the adoption of cloud technology is not very simple and seamless as it appears to be. Let's began with adoption challenges, virtualization of resources in IT began with the arrival of cloud computing, enterprise business applications, services and data started to be modernized to take on to this journey but this evolution introduced some complexities where the orchestration became more complicated as it started to transform IT structure into virtual systems, interdependency on network performance grew big and business models started to move towards pay as you go licensing as opposed to per instance [22].

NIST identified the following characteristics that every cloud service must have [23]:

1. It must be an on-demand self-service in which a customer can self-provision compute, store, etc., without human interaction.

2. It must contain broad network access with reachability and platform options (including thin and thick clients, phones, and tablets).

3. It must be a multi-tenant environment fostering location-independence.

4. It must support rapid elasticity with the ability to grow and shrink based on policy, with no impact to applications or users.

5. It must be a measured service, metered by performance with a pay-as-you-go pricing model.

There are six deployment models existing in a cloud platform: Public (bills on per hour or per month basis, open for public), Private (more expensive, better security, owned privately), Community (shared among users having common interests in organization) and Hybrid (mix of public, private or community). There are two emerging deployment models [24]: Federated (allows inter-cloud resources sharing and combined provisioning) and Intercloud (provides a basis for provisioning heterogeneous multi-provider cloud based project oriented infrastructures on-demand). Also there are three popular service models in cloud computing: Infrastructure as a

4

service (IaaS), Platform as a Service (PaaS) and Software as a Service (SaaS). Also there are two emerging service models in cloud computing: Data Analytics as a Service and HPC/Grid as a Service. The point is to carefully choose service model, deployment model and the service provider keeping your requirement and security needs in mind. Whatever data you store on a cloud platform will always be owned by you but it is stored by cloud service provider. So understanding data retention policy by the service provider is very important. Copying data from previous provider to new provider is needed to be done by you while shifting cloud provider. This makes compliance laws and policy to be clearly stated and understood by both the parties. So policies regarding deletion of any data or data retention will have to be stated and clarified while opting your service provider.

DDoS Attacks in Cloud

Cloud environment covers services right from the core infrastructure to software like email at an individual user level. This also brings enormous opportunities for individuals and organizations to host as well as use the services; there are a number of organizations offering different types of cloud services. By implementing cloud the organizations certainly gets the benefit of reduced capital investment, faster implementation cycle with net reduction in hardware-software procurement and installation and thus many miss out on the fact that responsibility to abide to the regulatory requirements imposed by various federal agencies and regulatory bodies is still with them. Non-conformance to the regulation might attract huge penalties and in cases federal agencies can also revoke the organizations licence to operate. Cloud Environment is vulnerable to attacks. One of the most popular attacks is Distributed Denial of Service (DDoS) attack. Some of the other attacks are Cloud Malware Injection attack, Side Channel attack, Authentication attack and Man in the Middle Cryptographic attack. DDoS attacks have become a common means for cybercriminals to distract a target's security, said Akamai's senior security advocate Martin McKeay [12]. Hackers are increasingly turning to distributed denial-of-service (DDoS) attacks to take companies offline or steal their sensitive data, according to a new report from Corero Network Security [14]. In table 1 and table 2 some of the major DDoS Attacks have been stated from year 1998 to 2018. The most surprising part of these DDoS is that the intensity of attacks have been increasing. The more ubiquitous the technology being adopted like Internet of Things (IoT) and Artificial Intelligence, the reach of these DDoS attacks are more widespread.

Year	DDoS Attacks in the past
1998	First DDoS tools were discovered. These tools were not used widely but point-to-point DoS attacks and Smurf amplification attacks continued.
1999	A trinoo network was used to flood a single system at the University of Minnessota, which made the network unusable for more than 2 days. And massive attack using Shaft was detected. The Data gathered during the attack was then analyzed in early 2000 by Sven Dietrich and presented in a paper at the USENIX LISA 2000 conference.
2000	15 year old boy Michael Calce (Mafiaboy) launched attack on Yahoo's website. He was then sentenced in juvenile detention center for 8months. He also went forward to degrade the servers of CNN, eBay, Dell, and Amazon, showing how easy it was to damage such major websites.
2001	The attack size grows from Mbps to Gbps. Efnet was affected by a 3 Gbps DDoS attack.
2002	It was reported that 9 of the 13 root internet servers were under serious threat of DDoS attack. Congestion due to attack made few root name servers were not reachable from many parts of the global Internet, which made many valid queries unanswered.
2003	Mydoom was used to shut down the service of SCO group's website. Thousands of PC's were infected to send the data to target server.

2004	Authorize-IT and 2Checkout were Online payment processing firms attacked by DDoS in April targeted. It was later known that the attackers extorted and threatened to shut down there sites.
2005	In August of 2005, jaxx.de, a gambling site was under DDoS attack and to stop this attack, the attacker demanded 40,000 euros.
2006	In December 2007 during the riots in Russia, government sites suffered severe DDoS attacks. Access to IP addresses outside Estonia was removed by many of them for several days.
2007	In December 2007 during the riots in Russia, government sites suffered severe DDoS attacks. Access to IP addresses outside Estonia was removed by many of them for several days.
2008	In November 2008, the Conficker worm used vulnerabilities found in Microsoft OS. It uses vulnerable machine and other machines are unwillingly connected to it, to make a large botnet.
2009	On 4th July (Independence Day in the US) 27 websites of White House, Federal Trade Commission, Department of Transportation, and the Department of the Treasury were attacked. On 1st august, Blogging pages of many social networking sites (Twitter, Facebook etc.) were affected by DDoS attack, aimed at "Cyxymu" Georgian blogger.
2010	Operation Payback: DDoS attacks launched on websites of MasterCard, PayPal and Visa, as they decide to stop giving service to WikiLeaks.
2011	LulzSec hacktivist group attacked website of CIA (cia.gov).
2012	Many attacks at us banks involve use of itsoknoproblembro DDoS tool. Many such do-it-yourself toolkits are available.

2013	150 Gbps DDoS attacks are increasing

Table1: DDoS attacks in past [3] (Source: "Understanding DDoS Attack & Its Effect In Cloud Environment" by Rashmi V. Deshmukha , Kailas K. Devadkarb published in Elsvier Procedia Computer Science 49 (2015) 202 – 210)

Year	DDoS Attacks in the Past
2014	400Gbps attack, that was reported to Arbor by a third party and the firm was not able to confirm many details beyond its imposing size [11]
2015	In the quarter there were also 12 attacks that were categorized as "mega attacks," peaking at more than 1,000 gigabits per second (Gbps) and 50 million packets per second (Mpps) [12].
2016	Dyn (company that controls much of the internet's domain name system (DNS) infrastructure) was hit on 21 October and remained under sustained assault for most of the day, bringing down sites including Twitter, the Guardian, Netflix, Reddit, CNN and many others in Europe and the US [13].
2017	In Q3 2017, organizations experienced an average of 237 DDoS attack attempts per month—or eight per day, the report found. These numbers represent a 35% increase in monthly attack attempts from Q2, and a whopping 91% increase from Q1. [14]
2018	The bank ABN Amro became the first victim on Saturday, while Rabobank and ING Bank were hit on Monday, along with the Dutch Taxation Authority [15].

Table2: DDoS attacks 2014-2018

During this period increase in Ransom Denial of Service (RDoS) is seen on rise where the attackers send a message to victim demanding ransom in bitcoins which if not paid will result in sensitive data loss. RDoS attacks returned in Q3 2017, as this method allows cybercriminals to extort money from their victims [14]. The growing availability in DDoS-for-hire services and the proliferation of unsecured Internet of Things (IoT) devices has led to the increase in DDoS attacks in 2017-Corero Network Security, 2017 [14].

Kaspersky Lab's did IT security survey in 2017. It polled 5,200 business representatives from 29 countries. The survey pointed at financial implications of reacting to DDoS attacks has resulted in $123,000 for SMBs per incident in 2017, compared to $106,000 in 2016.When asked about the specific consequences experienced as a result of a DDoS attack, most organizations (33%) claim that the cost incurred in fighting the attack and restoring services is the main burden, while a quarter (25%) cited money spent investing in an offline or back-up system while online services are unavailable, 23% stated that a loss of revenue and business opportunities occurred as a direct result of DDoS attacks, whereas 22% listed the loss of reputation among clients and partners as another direct consequence of a DDoS attack [16].

Blockchain for Cloud

Distribution of digital information which cannot be copied is the essence of Blockchain technology. Blockchain has (a) Data: Value of transaction attached to the block which includes From, To and Amount (b) Hash Code: Special code for every transaction (c) Hash of Previous Block. The amazing feature of this technology is that it doesn't have centralized record keeping as it is hosted by millions of computers at the same time. The data is available to anyone on the internet and beyond the scope of hacking. Due to decentralized nature direct modification of data is not possible. Instead of shared ledger system used by banks, distributed ledger system should be used which gets automatically updated with any change on the current available version and the updated version is made available to all in the network. Two users of the same document cannot mess with the same document/record at the same time. As a peer-to-peer network, combined with a distributed time-stamping server, Blockchain databases can be managed autonomously to exchange information between disparate parties [21]. Here the users are the administrators and data once entered in a block cannot be altered. Public Blockchain allows anyone in the network to see or send transactions as long as they are part of the process of transaction or any other activity. Private Blockchains, in contrast, restrict the ability to write to a distributed ledger to one organization, such as a group of employees within a corporation, or between a set number of organizations, such as a number of banks that agree to a network partnership [21].

Blockchain DDoS attacks [18] can be made to happen if 1c or 100$ transactions blocks are initiated multiple times. The transaction cost for 1c and 100$ is same and so with multiple 1c block transactions Blockchain DDoS attacks can be done which will lead to transaction loss and useless occupancy of resources. So multiple such blocks will have negative impact resulting in Blockchain DDoS attacks.

DDoS attacks can be avoided by opting for these mentioned solutions: (a) By using Blockchain, Maryland-based Gladius is creating a system that would allow people to rent out their unused bandwidth so that it can be used to absorb malicious DDoS traffic and mitigate against attacks [17]. (b) The other alternate way is to use dynamic trust management method (DTMM) of Organic Network in a Private Blockchain Network. (c) Third robust alternative can be to combine the above two solutions given in (a) and (b). In the following work DTMM is being discussed in detail and how it can improve cloud experience by avoiding DDoS attacks and also Blockchain DDoS attacks.

Organic Networks – merger of 'viral and social' networks [20]

The subject (or topic of organic networks) came into existence due to the merger of two distinct bodies of research that have been proceeding independently in the Media Lab for past several years. They are:

1. Viral Networks
2. Influence Networks

Viral Networks

The term "viral" is an observable event that keeps on changing. Viral phenomena are replicative in nature. This implies that viral phenomena are objects or patterns that are able to replicate themselves or convert other objects or patterns into copies of it when these objects are exposed to them.

Influence Networks

As stated by Lippman and Pentland (2004), innovation is defined by society, and not by technology. This is the overriding premise of organic networks. The networks build due to social contact and influence are called influence networks. A prime example can be Wi-Fi and an ad hoc, hotspot based Wi-Fi network.

Organic Networks are "next generation networks" and have self *x properties. Dynamic trust management method is the heart of Organic Networks, where the trust value gets updated according to the performance of the node [20]. The performance analysis of the node will be based on information transaction and trust level of an individual node. It will not depend on recommendation or certificates. The node identification will be done both at the system and individual level.

Using Private Blockchain with DTMM in Cloud Platform

In dynamic trust management method (DTMM) trust value gets updated according to the performance of the node. The performance analysis of the node will be based on information transaction and trust level of an individual node. It will not depend on recommendation or certificates. The node identification will be done at the system and individual level. So organizations opting for Cloud Technology can put their requirement for a Private Blockchain Network with DTMM for network/node authentication for security reasons. The data here will be stored and updated in blocks with restricted and secure access.

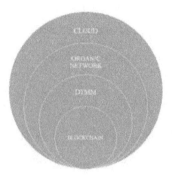

Figure 1: Cloud Technology for Organizations

Here dynamic trust management method (DTMM) has been proposed in Figure 2, where the trust value gets updated according to the performance of the node. The performance analysis of the node will be based on information transaction and trust level of an individual node. It will not depend on recommendation or certificates. The node identification will be done at the organizational, system and individual level. For individual level identification both personal and professional level details would be required and access would differ from person to person. The node identification and registration would be category based and will consist of unique identification number (Eg. Aadhaar Card), system identification number, country, state, organization (small, medium, large, global, national and/school, college, companies-government, public, private), individual, purpose, Trust Level and Task. Organizations can add or remove the categories from the list of requirements for node identification and registration as per their need and security level. If the country is same then node is not taken as new node. But if one moves from one country to another then existing node will be considered as a new node. In such a situation, system identification will be a must. If a node is already present on the network then the details of the previous transactions and search details will be available. If it is a new node, it will have to register first and will be given a trust level to enter the node initially. Network management policy would exist at node level, network level and mission level. The node will be always measured throughout its usage time for security and authentication reasons.

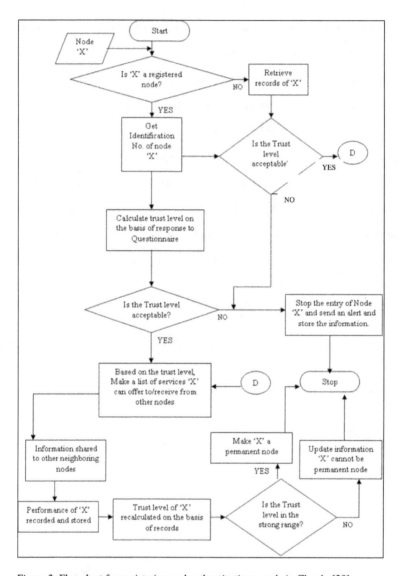

Figure 2: Flowchart for registering and authenticating a node in Cloud   [20]

In a Private Blockchain environment using DTMM in a cloud platform would make it secure and scalable. Suppose a user is trying to access some confidential data from a bank in a cloud environment. The user will have to enter the network which is a Private Blockchain network as

14

the information needed is confidential. The user may have an account in the bank and is an existing customer. So the user is a registered user and its trust value is calculated based on current response and past record. The services available and the information access is granted which may not allow it to access confidential data of the bank. So if the user/customer tries to get those confidential data, an alert will be sent across the network and the trust level will be updated on the basis of performance. The user/customer may be disconnected from the network immediately or it may be dropped out from availing any future services. Depending on the data breech needful actions can be taken. Current Trust Value will be: Trust value = (trust value of questionnaire) + (past node performance) + (present node performance)

The performance history of the node/user "X" is checked and trust value is updated based on its past performance and is compared with the following baselines range

1. Level 1 : less than 40%

2. Level 2 : 40% to 50%

3. Level 3 : 50 to 60%

4. Level 4 : 60% to 70%

5. Level 5 : 70% to 80%

6. Level 6 : 80% to 90%

7. Level 7 : Greater than 90%

Using a pre-defined mapping of trust level and the list of services, information is shared in the network with the member nodes in blocks as what services the node/user "X" can offer or avail. No reference is required as it is based on system and the individuals on the system to prove their identity. Here option of special access can be added for sudden or emergency situation depending solely on the provider and user under agreed format.

15

Here input to the algorithm would be "Node/user that wants to get access" and the output of the algorithm is the "acceptance of node/user" or "rejection of node/user". Level 1 being the weakest trust level, in which the node is even barred to join the network after initial trust level assessment as a potential threat is seen. With the increasing trust level the services a node can avail/provide also increases. If a nodes trust level lies in level 7 then it can be made permanent node else not. Also verification of permanent node will be done on a periodic basis depending on the sensitivity of information. Even punishments related to data breach can be clearly stated with details of the user existing along with digital signatures. In case of new node/user firstly authentication and KYC (Know Your Customer) or Know Your User (KYU) details will have to be inline before availing any services. The trust level will be stored and circulated in blocks along with past services record for easy reference and security.

No certificate is needed; trust value is the baseline for proving the creditability of the node/user. The initial registration only provides the basic authorization to the node for joining the network; however, its trust level will be responsible for the services the node/user can avail. The higher the trust level, the higher is service authorization level.

Compliance in Cloud

Data security, authenticity, privacy and reliability are some of the most sensitive and ethical issues. The data of all the cloud users has to be secured for privacy and protection. How safe are we in the cloud environment? What are the cloud service provider's security measures and what are their security standards? The legal and compliance challenges raised due to the stated challenges and concerns are still most important. When you tend to move data to an external environment for storage or backup, the first thought that comes to mind is the safety, privacy and originality of data stored in that external environment. When you move to a cloud platform, carefully check the security and compliance policy of the cloud service provider. Regulation are set of policies laid out to safeguard the use of sensitive business data and private data. The main intent of these regulations are to protect consumers' privacy and provide security by enforcing attributes such as confidentiality, integrity, availability, and accountability (CIAA) [5]. Compliance is needed to enforce rules for complying with the policies defined in the regulations. Because of the very nature of cloud technology, compliance is a shared responsibility among organizations and service providers; it involves service providers, service brokers, customers, and auditors [5].

You have to be careful when Service Level Agreements (SLA's) are being formulated between you and the cloud service provider to maintain compliance in cloud. All SLA's should be formulated as per current laws and industry standards. The main question that you should ask while choosing your cloud service provider are [7]:

    a. Where is our data going to reside?

    b. Who is going to look after it?

    c. Who is going to be able to see it?

    d. Is it going to be the people that manage the infrastructure for us?

    e. Is it going to be internal and external people?

    f. And if we use a public cloud how secure is that cloud platform for us?

g. Is the cloud going to be segregated from other organizations' data?

h. How is it being secured on the cloud?

Data Protection Laws in India

The national law regulating the collection and use of personal data is the Information Technology Act 2000 (IT Act) [8]. Though IT acts stand on violations committed outside India and relatable punishments have not been clearly stated but the law is applicable for whole of India. Any person that is negligent in using reasonable security practices and procedures (RSPPs) in protecting sensitive personal data or information (SPDI) is liable to pay compensation for any wrongful loss or wrongful gain (section 43A, IT Act) [8].

Rule 7 Under IT Act (2000) states regulations for Retention of electronic records as per IT Act[10]—(1) Where any law provides that documents, records or information shall be retained for any specific period, then, that requirement shall be deemed to have been satisfied if such documents, records or information are retained in the electronic form, if— (a) the information contained therein remains accessible so as to be usable for a subsequent reference; (b) the electronic record is retained in the format in which it was originally generated, sent or received or in a format which can be demonstrated to represent accurately the information originally generated, sent or received; (c) the details which will facilitate the identification of the origin, destination, date and time of dispatch or receipt of such electronic record are available in the electronic record: Provided that this clause does not apply to any information which is automatically generated solely for the purpose of enabling an electronic record to be dispatched or received. (2) Nothing in this section shall apply to any law that expressly provides for the retention of documents, records or information in the form of electronic records.

Rule 85 Under IT Act (2000) lists Offences by companies [10]-(1) Where a person committing a contravention of any of the provisions of this Act or of any rule, direction or order made thereunder is a company, every person who, at the time the contravention was committed, was in charge of, and was responsible to, the company for the conduct of business of the company as well as the company, shall be guilty of the contravention and shall be liable to be proceeded against and punished accordingly: Provided that nothing contained in this sub-section shall render any such person liable to punishment if he proves that the contravention took place without his knowledge or that he exercised all due diligence to prevent such contravention. (2) Notwithstanding anything contained in sub-section (1), where a contravention of any of the provisions of this Act or of any rule, direction or order made thereunder has been committed by a company and it is proved that the contravention has taken place with the consent or connivance of, or is attributable to any neglect on the part of, any director, manager, secretary or other officer of the company, such director, manager, secretary or other officer shall also be deemed to be guilty of the contravention and shall be liable to be proceeded against and punished accordingly. Explanation–For the purposes of this section,– (i) "company" means anybody corporate and includes a firm or other association of individuals; and (ii) "director", in relation to a firm, means a partner in the firm.

Rule 75 Under IT Act (2000) has to apply for offence or contravention committed outside India [10]–(1) Subject to the provisions of sub-section (2), the provisions of this Act shall apply also to any offence or contravention committed outside India by any person irrespective of his nationality. (2) For the purposes of sub-section (1), this Act shall apply to an offence or contravention committed outside India by any person if the act or conduct constituting the offence or contravention involves a computer, computer system or computer network located in India.

Rule 72 Under IT Act (2000) states Penalty for Breach of confidentiality and privacy[10] –Save as otherwise provided in this Act or any other law for the time being in force, if any person who, in pursuance of any of the powers conferred under this Act, rules or regulations made thereunder, has secured access to any electronic record, book, register, correspondence, information, document or other material without the consent of the person concerned discloses such electronic record, book, register, correspondence, information, document or other material to any other person shall be punished with imprisonment for a term which may extend to two years, or with fine which may extend to one lakh rupees, or with both.

All these regulations listed above clearly convey a strong message regarding the IT laws relating to protection of data and information inside and outside India.

The national laws regulating the collection and use of personal data is the Information Technology Act 2000(IT ACT) [8]. Though IT Acts stands on violations committed outside India, are not very clear, but laws are applicable for India. The IT Act (2000) talks on laws related to:

1. Digital Signature and Electronic Signature

2. Electronic Governance: Legal recognition, use, Delivery, retention, Audit, publication and contract validation   of electronic records

3. Attribution, acknowledgement, and dispatch of electronic records

4. Secure Electronic records and secure electronic signature

5. Regulation of certifying authorities

6. Electronic Signature certificates: Certifying , representation, suspension, revocation of Digital Signature Certificates

7. Duties of subscribers

8. Penalties, Compensation and Adjudication: it covers penalty and compensation to computers etc., failure to protect data, failure to furnish information, residual penalty etc.

9. Under offenses section, more than twenty four types of offenses have been listed and punishments related to that.

10. Exemption of Intermediaries in certain cases

11. Rules on Examiner of Electronic Evidence

12. Miscellaneous section with states rules on Acts to have an overriding effect, Protection of action, offenses by companies, Central and State Government powers to make rules and Power of controller etc.

Approach for Managing Compliance in Cloud: India

For organizations moving towards cloud solutions or already using cloud solutions have a trade-off of external dependency and exposure as compared to in-house IT. And with external parties involved to meet the compliance there is a need to have the expectations set and assessed. Organizations need to have a compliance management policy implemented ahead of time; in fact this policy should be one of the inputs and considerations for the organizations for selecting the cloud service provider, while signing an agreement with the service provider. With important business process and data exposed over internet and involvement of an external solution partner, information security becomes crucial and should be included in the compliance management policy. One has to verify which compliance guidelines the service provider is using and what are the chances of e-discovery? Also clarity on incidence response plan has to be in case of situations of data mishandling or data leak.

Companies opting cloud services should clearly ask for these to be stated in SLAs from the service providers.

1. Which Cloud Technology are they using? Does it include Blockchain Technology in cloud environment?

2. How safe is the cloud environment to store and retrieve sensitive data?

3. Who is the intermediary?

4. Will the intermediary change?

5. Will the contract be valid incase the intermediary change?

6. Details about team members on your project?

7. Any change to be notified immediately and same to come into effect on the SLA and compliance policies.

8. To rule out chance of escape under Rule85 which states that nothing contained in this sub-section shall render any such person liable to punishment if he proves that the contravention took place without his knowledge for that he exercised all due diligence to prevent such contravention.

   Organization should clearly state that any such incident accounting to financial or reputation or sensitive information loss will result in the service provider to compensate the service buyer depending on the extent of damage

9. Rule 7 under IT Act (2000) encourages the possibility of retention or storage of data/information in support of any law that expressly provides for the retention of documents, records or information inform of electronic records. Hence the organizations will have to check their documents, data, records or information to rule out the possibility of contradicting with any existing law that expressly provides for their retention. This should be clearly stated in SLA.

10. As per Rule 85 under IT Act (2000) there is no clear punishments in breaches as it is dependent on guilt. So organizations will have to clearly state out clause and compensation relating to information or security breach.

11. Rule75 IT Act (2000) is valid for any offense made by a computer, computer system or computer network located in India or by a person staying in India. There is no mention about offense being done from outside India. So while designing SLAs this point will have to take into consideration by organization.

12. Rule72 under IT Act (2000) which states Penalty for Breach of confidentiality and privacy is small. What if an organization IPR related information just before filling? So the loss would be big. Accordingly the compensation should be big. So organizations will have to clearly state compensatory as per their loss.

The process flow and major steps of the approach for managing the compliance has been represented in the figure, which is based on the **Plan Do Check Act** principle.

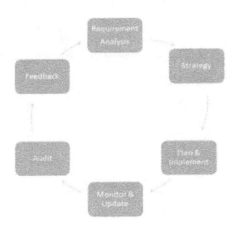

Figure 3: Approach for Managing Compliance in Cloud

It starts with developing a **Requirement Analysis**, which should cover the technology, deployment models, applicable standards, regulations and even the best practices of the Industry. This needs to be aligned with organizations **Strategic** plan, and should cover the performance standards, privacy, applications and services along with security aspects. The areas when drilled down should cover the compliance requirements of the business process, the business units and even the employees of the organizations who are exposed on the cloud.

In **Planning** stage the responsibilities of parties involved (i.e. service provider, user, customer), the expectations, assumptions and also the frequency of audits for meeting the requirements is charted out. The emphasis here should be on drawing clear lines on the responsibility and expectations with cloud provider. Also guidelines for opting for Smart Contracts can be laid down in this phase. So after complete **Plan** is laid out, one should move towards the **Implement**

23

phase. Constant monitoring of the process, policies and fulfilment of the requirements should be done in **Monitor and Update** phase. **Audit** is an integral part of the process to check if all the earlier actions have been carefully and perfectly executed. The feedback obtained from the Audit phase will be sent as **Feedback** to the First phase that is the **Requirement and Analysis** phase for improvement or updates if needed. All these phases should be followed as practiced in any standard quality management of compliance for organizations to prevent data theft and loss. The feedback is essential to close the findings of audits and observations while monitoring the processes.

Organizations may adopt different models and approach, however while designing a compliance management framework or system especially related to data storage, special emphasis should be given to the below mentioned conflicting aspects:

1. Data Collection Limitation and its usage

2. Retention and Destruction of data

3. Limitation of Private and Personal data usage and transfer

4. Transfer of data with permission and protection

5. Accountability

A well drafted compliance policy when implemented will create an environment of self-accountability and minimize risks thus enabling organizations to focus more towards end products and services resulting in a satisfied customer and improved business results. Organizations should opt for Smart Contracts for Cloud Compliance with the Cloud Service Providers because it can digitally be updated and is available in the network for users of the network. It should be available in form of blocks and available on the network. Depending on the authorization and trust level, services and information will be viewable. Figure 4 illustrates a simple cloud model which includes Blockchain Technology, DTMM, Services, Cloud Compliance and secure service in Cloud platform.

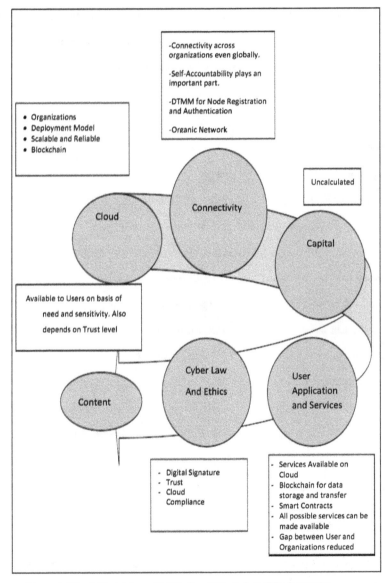

Figure 4: Cloud Model to avoid DDoS and Blockchain DDoS Attacks

Cloud Model given will help the cloud providers to provide DDoS and Blockchain DDoS Attack free services along with automatic compliance designing and management based on organizational need. Applications can be developed by the cloud service provider based on Models and Services being offered in a Private Blockchain technology having additional features like ON and DTMM, cloud compliance, Smart Contracts (computer protocol intended to digitally facilitate, verify, or enforce the negotiation or performance of a contract [25]), Regulations and others as per requirement.

Conclusion

Cloud computing is not just a technology breakthrough; it is also a business innovation and provides economic benefit by resource sharing and collaborations. Cloud Computing has provided a platform to other businesses to leverage technology at a reasonable pricing. The customers of cloud need to remember that the responsibility of meeting federal regulation and standards still lies with them. Compliance management not only would come handy in meeting the regulatory requirements but will also help them in managing organizational risks and even selecting their cloud partners in a market which will soon be flooded with options. The cloud service providers should also include compliance as a part of the operational process in order to ease global integration, avoid vendor conflicts, support transparency between users and providers, diverse regulations of countries, and to efficiently handle risks thus resulting in competitive advantage. Organic networks can also be called as "the next generation networks". The idea of decentralized data-sharing applications, group information sharing and packet voice will become tenets. Routing, relaying, signal regeneration, flow control and error control will be embodied in each node (or end system). The user will not require permission to join the workgroup and no password or login will be needed. An end system or node should be an adaptive system. An adaptive system is able to adapt its behaviour according to changes in its environment or to the changes in the parts of the system itself. The existence and termination of sessions would be possible at the nodes. Summarizing the above statements, it can be said that, intelligence should be at the node or end system and the system should scale without bounds where each node adds capacity. By adopting DTMM or switching to Organic Network platform along with Blockchain Technology, adoption of cloud can be made widespread and seamless. Also it will be able to resolve the below mentioned problems

- Security and privacy

- Controllability and flexibility

- Visibility and availability

- Auditability and accountability

- Performance

- Compliance

It will thus be able to provide secure platform for its users and organizations. Also the replicative, self-organizing, decentralized and intelligent end systems or nodes should corroborate adaptive communication where the communication system, automatically uses feedback information obtained from the system itself or from the signals carried by the system to modify dynamically system operational parameters to attain win-win agreement. These scalable, adaptive, viral and social networks (called organic networks), have to be managed. Thus organizations will have to work in this direction to make it a reality.

References

1. https://pdfs.semanticscholar.org/95c0/ae8181bbd949b69d23b5672038fdf4e4a3d7.pdf :
   DoD 2nd Feb'18
2. http://www.iscturkey.org/assets/files/2016/03/2013-paper46.pdf : DoD 2nd Feb'18
3. https://ac.els-cdn.com/S1877050915007541/1-s2.0-S1877050915007541-
   main.pdf?_tid=99b04462-0818-11e8-ab14-
   00000aacb362&acdnat=1517576418_00f7acacaa9d865cc17eb4f1b8500653 : DoD 2nd
   Feb'18
4. http://paper.ijcsns.org/07_book/201212/20121217.pdf : DoD 2nd Feb'18
5. https://jisajournal.springeropen.com/articles/10.1186/s13174-016-0046-8 : DoD 9th
   Feb'18
6. Manisha Kumari Deep, "Managing Compliance in Cloud", Corporate Talk Magazine,
   2012.
7. http://www.computerweekly.com/podcast/Cloud-compliance-What-it-is-and-how-to-
   achieve-it : DoD 9th Feb'18
8. https://content.next.westlaw.com/Document/I02064fb41cb611e38578f7ccc38dcbee/View/
   FullText.html?contextData=(sc.Default)&transitionType=Default&firstPage=true&bhcp=
   1 : DoD 13th Feb'18
9. http://www.wipo.int/edocs/lexdocs/laws/en/in/in099en.pdf :DoD 13th Feb'18
10. http://lawmin.nic.in/ld/P-ACT/2000/A2000-21.pdf : DoD 13th Feb'18
11. https://www.techworld.com/news/security/worlds-largest-ddos-attack-reached-400gbps-
    says-arbor-networks-3595715/ : DoD 25th Feb'18
12. https://www.digitaltrends.com/computing/ddos-attacks-hit-record-numbers-in-q2-2015/ :
    DoD 25th Feb'18
13. https://www.theguardian.com/technology/2016/oct/26/ddos-attack-dyn-mirai-botnet :
    DoD 25th Feb'18
14. https://www.techrepublic.com/article/ddos-attacks-increased-91-in-2017-thanks-to-iot/ :
    DoD 25th Feb'18
15. http://www.zdnet.com/article/ddos-mystery-whos-behind-this-massive-wave-of-attacks-
    targeting-dutch-banks/ : DoD 25th Feb'18
16. http://ddosattacks.net/ddos-costs-skyrocket-for-smbs-and-enterprises-alike/ : DoD 25th
    Feb'18
17. https://www.inc.com/joseph-steinberg/could-blockchain-technology-end-ddos-
    attacks.html : DoD 26th Feb'18

18. https://www.youtube.com/watch?v=IehHwBt3NAg : DoD 26th Feb'18

19. Manisha Kumari Deep, "Blockchain Technology for avoiding $1.77 Billion Scam in Public Banks: India", **ISBN:** 1230002174112, www.kobo.com , February 2018

20. Manisha Kumari Deep and Gadadhar Sahoo, "Organic IT Infrastructure Planning and Implementation", **ISBN-10:** 9352740726 **ISBN-13:** 978-9352740727, Published by Lakshmi Publication, December 2017. https://www.amazon.in/Organic-Infrastructure-Planning-Implementation-Manisa/dp/9352740726/ref=sr_1_1?s=books&ie=UTF8&qid=1519650109&sr=1-1&keywords=organic+IT+infrastructure&dpID=51lxsMT1p0L&preST=_SY264_BO1,204,203,200_QL40_&dpSrc=srch : DoD 26th Feb'18

21. https://www.computerworld.com/article/3191077/security/what-is-blockchain-the-most-disruptive-tech-in-decades.html : DoD 27th Feb'18

22. Naqi Khan (Author), 2017, Cloud Computing. Adoption Challenges, Green operations, Private & Public implementations, Munich, GRIN Verlag, https://www.grin.com/document/367866

23. https://www.annese.com/characteristics-of-cloud-computing : DoD 4th March'18

24. https://cloudcomputing.ieee.org/images/files/education/studygroup/Cloud_Service_and_Deployment_Models.pdf : DoD 4th March'18

25. https://en.wikipedia.org/wiki/Smart_contract : DoD 13th March'18